Counting on GOD!

Multiplying Math Skills
with Spiritual Principles

Coretta Wren

Counting on God!

© 2006 Coretta Wren

All rights reserved. No part of this publication may be reproduced, stored in a retrieval system, or transmitted in any form or by any means – electronic, mechanical, photocopy, recording, or any other – except for brief quotations in printed reviews, without the prior permission of the publisher.

Know Me Publication
P. O. Box 21232
Auburn Hills, Michigan 48321
248-635-6200

wrenknowmepublication@yahoo.com

ISBN: 978-0-9790934-0-1

Cover and interior design by PriorityONE Publications

Printed in the United States of America

Directions:
Break the code by using the number chart below. Once you have broken the code, add, divide and reduce to lowest fraction and place in decimal form, subtract, identify on number line, multiple, and divide and find the lowest common fraction.

$\dfrac{A}{1}$ $\dfrac{B}{2}$ $\dfrac{C}{3}$ $\dfrac{D}{4}$ $\dfrac{E}{5}$ $\dfrac{F}{6}$ $\dfrac{G}{7}$ $\dfrac{H}{8}$ $\dfrac{I}{9}$

$\dfrac{J}{10}$ $\dfrac{K}{11}$ $\dfrac{L}{12}$ $\dfrac{M}{13}$ $\dfrac{N}{14}$ $\dfrac{O}{15}$ $\dfrac{P}{16}$ $\dfrac{Q}{17}$ $\dfrac{R}{18}$

$\dfrac{S}{19}$ $\dfrac{T}{20}$ $\dfrac{U}{21}$ $\dfrac{V}{22}$ $\dfrac{W}{23}$ $\dfrac{X}{24}$ $\dfrac{Y}{25}$ $\dfrac{Z}{26}$

Activity #1

$$\overline{\begin{array}{cccc} 1 & 19 & 9 & 1 \end{array}}$$

Addition:

1+ 19 + 9 +1= _____

Division: Divide the answer above by the number below.

_____ ÷ 4 = _____

Subtraction

1 − 19 − 9 − 1 = _____

Number Line: Find the answer on the number line.

Multiplication:

1 x 19 x 9 x 1= _____

Fraction: Convert the answer above into a fraction or decimal using the total number of books in the bible as the devisor.

_____ ÷ _____ = _____

Activity #2

$$\overline{718135}$$

Addition:

7+18+1+3+5= _____

Division: Divide the answer above by the number below.

_____ ÷ 5 = _____

Subtraction:

7 − 18 − 1 − 3 − 5 = _____

Number Line: Find on the number line.

Multiplication:

7 x 18 x 1 x 3 x 5 = _____

Fraction: Convert the answer above into a fraction or decimal using the total number of books in the bible as the devisor.

_____ ÷ _____ = _____

Activity #3

> _____
> 19 16 9 18 9 20

Addition:

19 + 16 + 9 + 18 + 9 + 20 =

Division: Divide the answer above by the number below.

$$\underline{\hspace{2cm}} \div 6 = \underline{\hspace{2cm}}$$

Subtraction:

19 − 16 − 9 − 18 − 9 − 20 = _____

Number Line: Find on Number line.

Multiplication:

19 x 16 x 9 x 18 x 9 x 20 = _____

Fraction: Convert the answer above into a fraction or decimal using the total number of books in the bible as the devisor.

$$\underline{\hspace{2cm}} \div \underline{\hspace{1.5cm}} = \underline{\hspace{2cm}}$$

Activity #4

$$\overline{20\ \ 8\ \ 18\ \ 15\ \ 14\ \ 5}$$

Addition:

20 + 8 + 18 + 15 + 14 + 5 = _____

Division: Divide the answer above by the number below.

_____ ÷ 6 = _____

Subtraction:

20 − 8 − 18 − 15 − 14 − 5 = _____

Number Line: Find the answer on the number line.

Multiplication:

20 x 8 x 18 x 15 x 14 x 5 = _____

Fraction: Convert the answer above into a fraction or decimal using the total number of books in the bible as the devisor.

_____ ÷ _____ = _____

Activity #5

_____
6 1 9 20 8 6 21 12

Addition:

6 + 1 + 9 + 20 + 8 + 6 + 21 + 12 = _____

Division: Divide the answer above by the number below.

_____ ÷ 8 = _____

Subtraction:

6 − 1 − 9 − 20 − 8 − 6 − 21 − 12 = _____

Number of Line: Find the answer on the number line.

Multiplication:

6 x 1 x 9 x 20 x 8 x 6 x 21 x 12 = _____

Fraction: Convert the answer above into a fraction or decimal using the total number of books in the bible as the devisor.

_____ ÷ _____ = _____

Activity #6

> 5 16 8 5 19 21 19

Addition:

5 + 16 + 8 + 5 + 19 + 21 + 19 = _____

Division: Divide the answer above by the number below.

_____ ÷ 7 = _____

Subtraction:

5 − 16 − 8 − 5 − 19 − 21 − 19 = _____

Number Line: Find the number on the number line.

Multiplication:

5 x 16 x 8 x 5 x 19 x 21 x 19 = _____

Fraction: Convert the answer above into a fraction or decimal using the total number of books in the bible as the devisor.

_____ ÷ _____ = _____

Activity #7

_____
8 1 14 4 12 5 19 20 9 3 11 19

Addition:

      8 + 1 + 14 + 12 + 5 + 19 + 20
      + 9 + 3 + 11 + 19 = _____

Division: Divide the answer above by the number below.

      _____ ÷ 11 = _____

Subtraction:

      8 − 1 − 14 − 12 − 5 − 19 − 20
      − 9 − 3 − 11 − 19 = _____

Number Line: Find answer on number line.

Multiplication:

8 x 1 x 14 x 12 x 5 x 19 x 20 x 9 x 3 x 11 x 19 = _____

Decimal: Convert the answer above into a decimal using the total number of books in the bible as the devisor.

      _____ ÷ _____ = _____

Activity #8

> 3 12 15 20 8 5 19

Addition:

3 + 12 + 15 + 20 + 8 + 5 + 19 =

Division: Divide the answer above by the number below.

_____ ÷ 7 = _____

Subtraction:

3 − 12 − 15 − 20 − 8 − 5 − 19 = _____

Number line: Find the number on the number line.

Multiplication:

3 x 12 x 15 x 20 x 8 x 5 x 19 = _____

Decimal: Convert the answer above into a decimal using the total number of books in the bible as the devisor.

_____ ÷ _____ = _____

Activity #9

_____
19 5 22 5 14

Addition:

19 + 5 + 22 + 5 + 14 = _____

Division: Divide the answer above by the number below.

_____ ÷ 5 = _____

Subtraction:

19 − 5 − 22 − 5 − 14 = _____

Number Line: Find the answer on the number line.

Multiplication:

19 x 5 x 22 x 5 x 4 = _____

Fraction: Convert the answer above into a fraction or decimal using the total number of books in the bible as the devisor.

_____ ÷ _____ = _____

Activity #10

$$\overline{}$$
6 21 18 14 1 3 5

Addition:

6 + 21 + 18 + 14 + 1 + 3 + 5 = _____

Division: Divide the answer above by the number below.

_____ ÷ 7 = _____

Subtraction:

6 − 21 − 18 − 14 − 1 − 3 − 5 = _____

Number Line: Find the number on the number line.

Multiplication:

6 x 21 x 18 x 14 x 1 x 3 x 5 = _____

Fraction: Convert the answer above into a fraction or decimal using the total number of books in the bible as the devisor.

_____ ÷ _____ = _____

Activity #11

$$\overline{19\ 21\ 20\ 8}$$

Addition:

$$18 + 21 + 20 + 8 = \underline{}$$

Division: Divide the answer above by the number below.

$$\underline{} \div 4 = \underline{}$$

Subtraction:

$$18 - 21 - 20 - 8 = \underline{}$$

Number Line: Find the answer on the number line.

Multiplication:

$$18 \times 21 \times 20 \times 8 = \underline{}$$

Fraction: Convert the answer above into a fraction or decimal using the total number of books in the bible as the devisor.

$$\underline{} \div \underline{} = \underline{}$$

Activity #12

$$\overline{13 \quad 1 \quad 18 \quad 25}$$

Addition:

13 + 1 + 18 + 25 = _____

Division: Divide the number of numbers with the total.

_____ ÷ 4 = _____

Subtraction:

13 − 1 − 18 − 25 = _____

Number Line: Find the number on the number line.

Multiplication:

13 x 1 x 18 x 25 = _____

Fraction: Convert the answer above into a fraction or decimal using the total number of books in the bible as the devisor.

_____ ÷ _____ = _____

Activity #13

$$\overline{13 \quad 15 \quad 19 \quad 5 \quad 19}$$

Addition:

13 + 15 + 19 + 5 + 19 = _____

Division: Divide the answer above by the number below.

_____ ÷ 5 = _____

Subtraction:

13 − 15 − 19 − 5 − 19 = _____

Number Line: Find answer on the number line.

Multiplication:

13 x 15 x 19 x 5 x 19 = _____

Fraction: Convert the answer above into a fraction or decimal using the total number of books in the bible as the devisor.

_____ ÷ _____ = _____

Activity #14

$$\overline{15\ 2\ 1\ 4\ 9\ 1\ 8}$$

Addition:

15 + 2 + 1 + 4 + 9 + 1 + 8 = _____

Division: Divide the answer above by the number below.

_____ ÷ 7 = _____

Subtraction:

15 − 2 − 1 − 4 − 9 − 1 − 8 = _____

Number Line: Find the answer on the number line.

Multiplication:

15 x 2 x 1 x 4 x 9 x 1 x 8 = _____

Fraction: Convert the answer above into a fraction or decimal using the total number of books in the bible as the devisor.

_____ ÷ _____ = _____

Activity #15

$$\overline{1 \quad 18 \quad 11}$$

Addition:

$$1 + 18 + 11 = \underline{}$$

Division: Divide the answer above by the number below.

$$\underline{} \div 3 = \underline{}$$

Subtraction:

$$1 - 18 - 11 = \underline{}$$

Number Line: Find the answer on the number line.

Multiplication:

$$1 \times 18 \times 11 = \underline{}$$

Fraction: Convert the answer above into a fraction or decimal using the total number of books in the bible as the devisor.

$$\underline{} \div \underline{} = \underline{}$$

Activity #16

$$\overline{10\ 5\ 19\ 21\ 19}$$

Addition:

10 + 5 + 19 + 21 + 19 = _____

Division: Divide the answer above by the number below.

_____ ÷ 5 = _____

Subtraction:

10 − 5 − 19 − 21 − 19 = _____

Number Line: Find the number on the number line.

Multiplication:

10 x 5 x 19 x 21 x 19 = _____

Fraction: Convert the answer above into a fraction or decimal using the total number of books in the bible as the devisor.

_____ ÷ _____ = _____

Activity #17

$$\overline{9\ \ 19\ \ 1\ \ 9\ \ 1\ \ 8}$$

Addition:

9 + 19 + 1 + 9 + 1 + 8 = _____

Division: Divide the answer above by the number below.

_____ ÷ 6 = _____

Subtraction:

9 – 19 – 1 – 9 – 1 – 8 = _____

Number Line: Find the answer on the number line.

Multiplication:

9 x 19 x 1 x 9 x 1 x 8 = _____

Fraction: Convert the answer above into a fraction or decimal using the total number of books in the bible as the devisor.

_____ ÷ _____ = _____

Activity #18

$$\overline{}$$
13 1 20 20 8 5 23

Addition:

13 + 1 + 20 + 20 + 8 + 5 + 23 = _____

Division: Divide the answer above by the number below.

_____ ÷ 7 = _____

Subtraction:

13 − 1 − 20 − 20 − 8 − 5 − 23 = _____

Number Line: Find the answer on the number line.

Multiplication:

13 x 1 x 20 x 20 x 8 x 5 x 23 = _____

Fraction: Convert the answer above into a fraction or decimal using the total number of books in the bible as the devisor.

_____ ÷ _____ = _____

Activity #19

$$8 \ 15 \ 19 \ 5 \ 1$$

Addition:

$$8 + 15 + 19 + 5 + 1 = \underline{\qquad}$$

Division: Divide the answer above by the number below.

$$\underline{\qquad} \div 5 = \underline{\qquad}$$

Subtraction:

$$8 - 15 - 19 - 5 - 1 = \underline{\qquad}$$

Number of Line: Find the answer on the number line.

Multiplication:

$$8 \times 15 \times 19 \times 5 \times 1 = \underline{\qquad}$$

Fraction: Convert the answer above into a fraction or decimal using the total number of books in the bible as the devisor.

$$\underline{\qquad} \div \underline{\qquad} = \underline{\qquad}$$

Activity #20

$$\overline{}$$
$$1\ 4\ 1\ 13$$

Addition:

$$1 + 4 + 1 + 13 = \underline{}$$

Division: Divide the answer above by the number below.

$$\underline{} \div 4 = \underline{}$$

Subtraction:

$$1 - 4 - 1 - 13 = \underline{}$$

Number Line: Find the answer on the number line.

Multiplication:

$$1 \times 4 \times 1 \times 13 = \underline{}$$

Fraction: Convert the answer above into a fraction or decimal using the total number of books in the bible as the devisor.

$$\underline{} \div \underline{} = \underline{}$$

Activity #21

$$\overline{}$$
5 26 5 11 9 5 12

Addition:

5 + 26 + 5 + 11 + 9 + 5 + 12 = _____

Division:

_____ ÷ 7 = _____

Subtraction:

5 − 26 − 5 − 11 − 9 − 5 − 12 = _____

Number Line: Find the answer on the number line.

Multiplication:

5 x 26 x 5 x 11 x 9 x 5 x 12 = _____

Fraction: Convert the answer above into a fraction or decimal using the total number of books in the bible as the devisor.

_____ ÷ _____ = _____

Activity #22

$$\overline{}$$
$$18\ \ 5\ \ 13\ \ 1\ \ 14\ \ 19$$

Addition:

18 + 5 + 13 + 1 + 14 + 19 = _____

Division: Divide the answer above by the number below.

_____ ÷ 6 = _____

Subtraction:

18 − 5 − 13 − 1 − 14 − 19 = _____

Number Line: Find the answer on the number line.

Multiplication:

18 x 5 x 13 x 1 x 14 x 19 = _____

Fraction: Convert the answer above into a fraction or decimal using the total number of books in the bible as the devisor.

_____ ÷ _____ = _____

Activity #23

$$\overline{10 \quad 15 \quad 19 \quad 5 \quad 16 \quad 8}$$

Addition:

10 + 15 + 19 + 16 + 8 = _____

Division: Divide the answer above by the number below.

_____ ÷ 5 = _____

Subtraction:

10 + 15 + 19 + 16 + 8 = _____

Number Line: Find answer on number line.

Multiplication:

10 x 15 x 19 x 16 x 8 = _____

Fraction: Convert the answer above into a fraction or decimal using the total number of books in the bible as the devisor.

_____ ÷ _____ = _____

Activity #24

$$\overline{}$$
16 19 1 12 13

Addition:

16 + 19 + 1 + 12 + 13 = _____

Division: Divide the answer above by the number below.

_____ ÷ 5 = _____

Subtraction:

16 − 19 − 1 − 12 − 13 = _____

Number Line: Find the number on the number line.

Multiplication:

16 x 19 x 1 x 12 x 13 = _____

Fraction: Convert the answer above into a fraction or decimal using the total number of books in the bible as the devisor.

_____ ÷ _____ = _____

Activity #25

$$\overline{1\ 2\ 1\ 8}$$

Addition:

$$1 + 2 + 1 + 8 = \underline{}$$

Division: Divide the total of numbers by the answer.

$$\underline{} \div 4 = \underline{}$$

Subtraction:

$$1 - 2 - 1 - 8 = \underline{}$$

Number Line: Find the number on the number line.

Multiplication:

$$1 \times 2 \times 1 \times 8 = \underline{}$$

Fraction: Convert the answer above into a fraction or decimal using the total number of books in the bible as the devisor.

$$\underline{} \div \underline{} = \underline{}$$

Activity #26

$$\overline{10\ \ 21\ \ 4\ \ 1\ \ 8}$$

Addition:

10 + 21 + 4 + 1 + 8 = _____

Division: Divide the answer above by the number below.

_____ ÷ 5 = _____

Subtraction:

10 − 21 − 4− 1 − 8 = _____

Number Line: Find the number on the number line.

Multiplication:

10 x 21 x 4 x 1 x 8 = _____

Fraction: Convert the answer above into a fraction or decimal using the total number of books in the bible as the devisor.

_____ ÷ _____ = _____

Activity #27

_____
10 15 8 14

Addition:

10 + 15 + 8 + 4 = _____

Division: Divide the answer above by the number below.

_____ ÷ 4 = _____

Subtraction:

10 − 15 − 8 − 4 = _____

Number Line: Find the answer on the number line.

Multiplication:

10 x 15 x 8 x 4 = _____

Fraction: Convert the answer above into a fraction or decimal using the total number of books in the bible as the devisor.

_____ ÷ _____ = _____

Activity #28

$$\overline{}$$
1 13 15 19

Addition:

1 + 13 + 15 + 19 = _____

Division: Divide the answer above by the number below.

_____ ÷ 4 = _____

Subtraction:

1 − 13 − 15 − 19 = _____

Number Line: Find the number on the number line.

Multiplication:

1 x 13 x 15 x 19 = _____

Fraction: Convert the answer above into a fraction or decimal using the total number of books in the bible as the devisor.

_____ ÷ _____ = _____

Animals in the Bible

Directions: Break the codes by using the number chart below. Once you have broken the code, add, divide and reduce to lowest fraction and place in decimal form, subtract, identify on number line, multiple, and divide and find the lowest common fraction. After which find the words in the puzzles.

$\frac{A}{1}$	$\frac{B}{2}$	$\frac{C}{3}$	$\frac{D}{4}$	$\frac{E}{5}$	$\frac{F}{6}$	$\frac{G}{7}$	$\frac{H}{8}$	$\frac{I}{9}$
$\frac{J}{10}$	$\frac{K}{11}$	$\frac{L}{12}$	$\frac{M}{13}$	$\frac{N}{14}$	$\frac{O}{15}$	$\frac{P}{16}$	$\frac{Q}{17}$	$\frac{R}{18}$
$\frac{S}{19}$	$\frac{T}{20}$	$\frac{U}{21}$	$\frac{V}{22}$	$\frac{W}{23}$	$\frac{X}{24}$	$\frac{Y}{25}$	$\frac{Z}{26}$	

Animals in the Bible

C	C	H	R	I	S
B	A	F	I	S	H
I	S	L	L	U	B
R	P	A	V	L	E
D	S	C	Q	E	Y
S	N	C	V	L	S
E	I	E	I	A	G
C	O	R	W	M	O
I	L	D	H	B	D
M	C	E	O	E	Z
E	A	L	R	T	A
L	E	G	S	F	E
B	W	A	E	L	C
I	E	E	D	W	R
B	J	A	W	O	O

Activity #31

$$\overline{3 \; 1 \; 12 \; 22 \; 5 \; 19}$$

Addition:

3 + 1 + 12 + 22 + 5 +12 = _____

Division: Divide the answer above by the number below.

_____ ÷ 6 = _____

Subtraction:

3 − 1 − 12 − 22 − 5 − 12 = _____

Multiplication:

3 x 12 x 22 x 5 x 12 = _____

Fraction: Convert the answer above into a fraction or decimal using the total number of books in the bible as the devisor.

_____ ÷ _____ = _____

Activity #32

$$\overline{}$$
$$3\ \ 1\ \ 12\ \ 6$$

Addition:

$3 + 1 + 12 + 6 = \underline{}$

Division: Divide the answer above by the number below.

$\underline{} \div 4 = \underline{}$

Subtraction:

$3 - 1 - 12 - 6 = \underline{}$

Multiplication:

$3 \times 1 \times 12 \times 6 = \underline{}$

Fraction: Convert the answer above into a fraction or decimal using the total number of books in the bible as the devisor.

$\underline{} \div \underline{} = \underline{}$

Activity #33

$$\overline{2\ \ 5\ \ 1\ \ 19\ \ 20}$$

Addition:

2 + 5 + 1 + 19 + 20 = _____

Division: Divide the answer above by the number below.

_____ ÷ 5 = _____

Subtraction:

2 − 5 − 1 − 19 − 20 = _____

Multiplication:

2 x 5 x 1 x 19 x 20 = _____

Fraction: Convert the answer above into a fraction or decimal using the total number of books in the bible as the devisor.

_____ ÷ _____ = _____

Activity #34

$$\overline{}\\ 2\ \ 9\ \ 18\ \ 4\ \ 19$$

Addition:

2 + 9 + 18 + 4 + 19 = _____

Division: Divide the answer above by the number below.

_____ ÷ 5 = _____

Subtraction:

2 − 9 − 18 − 4 − 19 = _____

Multiplication:

2 x 9 x 18 x 4 x 19 = _____

Fraction: Convert the answer above into a fraction or decimal using the total number of books in the bible as the devisor.

_____ ÷ _____ = _____

Activity #35

$$\overline{2\ \ 21\ \ 22\ \ 12\ \ 19}$$

Addition:

$2 + 21 + 22 + 12 + 19 =$ _____

Division: Divide the answer above by the number below.

_____ ÷ 5 = _____

Subtraction:

$2 - 21 - 22 - 12 - 19 =$ _____

Multiplication:

$2 \times 21 \times 22 \times 12 \times 19 =$ _____

Fraction: Convert the answer above into a fraction or decimal using the total number of books in the bible as the devisor.

_____ ÷ _____ = _____

Activity #36

$$\overline{}$$
$$4\ \ 15\ \ 7$$

Addition:

4 + 15 + 7 = _____

Division: Divide the answer above by the number below.

_____ ÷ 3 = _____

Subtraction:

4 − 15 − 7 = _____

Multiplication:

4 x 15 x 7 = _____

Fraction: Convert the answer above into a fraction or decimal using the total number of books in the bible as the devisor.

_____ ÷ _____ = _____

Activity #37

$$\overline{2\ \ 1\ \ 7\ \ 12\ \ 5}$$

Addition:

$$2 + 1 + 7 + 12 + 5 = \underline{\qquad}$$

Division: Divide the answer above by the number below.

$$\underline{\qquad} \div 5 = \underline{\qquad}$$

Subtraction:

$$2 - 1 - 7 - 12 - 5 = \underline{\qquad}$$

Multiplication:

$$2 \times 1 \times 7 \times 12 \times 5 = \underline{\qquad}$$

Fraction: Convert the answer above into a fraction or decimal using the total number of books in the bible as the devisor.

$$\underline{\qquad} \div \underline{\qquad} = \underline{\qquad}$$

Activity #38

$$\overline{5\ \ 23\ \ 5}$$

Addition:

$5 + 23 + 5 = $ _____

Division: Divide the answer above by the number below.

_____ $\div 3 = $ _____

Subtraction:

$5 - 23 - 5 = $ _____

Multiplication:

$5 \times 23 \times 5 = $ _____

Fraction: Convert the answer above into a fraction or decimal using the total number of books in the bible as the devisor.

_____ $\div$ _____ $=$ _____

Activity #39

$$\overline{6\ 9\ 19\ 8}$$

Addition:

$$6 + 9 + 19 + 8 = \underline{}$$

Division: Divide the answer above by the number below.

$$\underline{} \div 4 = \underline{}$$

Subtraction:

$$6 - 9 - 19 - 8 = \underline{}$$

Multiplication:

$$6 \times 9 \times 19 \times 8 = \underline{}$$

Fraction: Convert the answer above into a fraction or decimal using the total number of books in the bible as the devisor.

$$\underline{} \div \underline{} = \underline{}$$

Activity #40

$$\overline{8 \quad 15 \quad 18 \quad 19 \quad 5}$$

Addition:

8 + 15 + 18 + 19 + 5 = _____

Division: Divide the answer above by the number below.

_____ ÷ 5 = _____

Subtraction:

9 − 15 − 18 − 19 − 5 = _____

Multiplication:

9 x 15 x 18 x 19 x 5 = _____

Fraction: Convert the answer above into a fraction or decimal using the total number of books in the bible as the devisor.

_____ ÷ _____ = _____

Activity #41

$$\overline{10 \quad 1 \quad 23}$$

Addition:

10 + 1 + 23 = _____

Division: Divide the answer above by the number below.

_____ ÷ 3 = _____

Subtraction:

10 − 1 − 23 = _____

Multiplication:

10 x 1 x 23 = _____

Fraction: Convert the answer above into a fraction or decimal using the total number of books in the bible as the devisor.

_____ ÷ _____ = _____

Activity #42

_____
12 1 13 2

Addition:

12 + 1 + 13 + 2 = _____

Division: Divide the answer above by the number below.

_____ ÷ 4 = _____

Subtraction:

12 − 1 − 13 − 2 = _____

Multiplication:

12 x 1 x 13 x 2 = _____

Fraction: Convert the answer above into a fraction or decimal using the total number of books in the bible as the devisor.

_____ ÷ _____ = _____

Activity #43

$$\overline{12 \ \ 9 \ \ 15 \ \ 14 \ \ 19}$$

Addition:

12 + 9 + 15 + 14 + 19 = _____

Division: Divide the answer above by the number below.

_____ ÷ 5 = _____

Subtraction:

12 − 9 − 15 − 14 − 19 = _____

Multiplication:

12 x 9 x 15 x 14 x 19 = _____

Fraction: Convert the answer above into a fraction or decimal using the total number of books in the bible as the devisor.

_____ ÷ _____ = _____

Activity #44

$$\overline{13 \ 9 \ 3 \ 5}$$

Addition:

$$13 + 9 + 3 + 5 = \underline{\hspace{2cm}}$$

Division: Divide the answer above by the number below.

$$\underline{\hspace{2cm}} \div 4 = \underline{\hspace{2cm}}$$

Subtraction:

$$13 - 9 - 3 - 5 = \underline{\hspace{2cm}}$$

Multiplication:

$$13 \times 9 \times 3 \times 5 = \underline{\hspace{2cm}}$$

Fraction: Convert the answer above into a fraction or decimal using the total number of books in the bible as the devisor.

$$\underline{\hspace{2cm}} \div \underline{\hspace{1.5cm}} = \underline{\hspace{2cm}}$$
$$\underline{\hspace{1.5cm}}$$

Answer Sheets

Behind this page are the answers to activities within this booklet.

We decided to put them in just in case you get stumped.

But remember...

It's better when you do all you can to figure them out on your own.

In other words...

Don't peek!

Answers

Activity #1

$$\frac{\text{A S I A}}{\text{1 19 9 1}}$$

Addition:

1+ 19 + 9 +1= **30**

Division:

30 ÷ 4 = **7.5 or 7½**

Subtraction:

1 – 19 – 9 – 1 = **-28**

Number Line: Find the answer on the number line.

Multiplication:

1 x 19 x 9 x 1 = **171**

Fraction: Place answer in a fraction. The bottom number is the total number books in the bible.

171 ÷ 66 = **2 39/66 or 2 13/22**

Answers

Activity #2

G	R	A	C	E
7	18	1	3	5

Addition:

7 + 18 + 1 + 3 + 5 = **34**

Division: divide 5 by the answer,

34 ÷ 5 = **6.8 or 6 4/5**

Subtraction:

7 − 18 − 1 − 3 − 5 = **-20**

Number Line: Find on the number line.

Multiplication:

7 x 18 x 1 x 3 x 5 = **1890**

Fraction or Decimals: Place answer in a fraction. The bottom number is the total number books in the bible.

1890 ÷ 66 = **28.63 or 28 42/66 or 28 7/11**

Answers

Activity #3

S	P	I	R	I	T
19	16	9	18	9	20

Addition:

19 + 16 + 9 + 18 + 9 + 20 = **91**

Division:

91 ÷ 6 = **15.16 and 15 1/6**

Subtraction:

19 − 16 − 9 − 18 − 9 − 20 = **-53**

Number Line: Find on Number line.

Multiplication:

19 x 16 x 9 x 18 x 9 x 20 = **8,864,640**

Fractions: Divide the answer above by the total number of books in the bible.

8,864,640 ÷ 66 = 134312.73 or 134,312 48/66 or 134,312 8/11

Answers

Activity #4

T H R O N E
20 8 18 15 14 5

Addition:

20 + 8 + 18 + 15 + 14 + 5 = **80**

Division:

80 ÷ 6 = **13.3**

Subtraction:

20 − 8 − 18 − 15 − 14 − 5 = **−40**

Number Line: Find the answer on the number line.

Multiplication:

20 x 8 x 18 x 15 x 14 x 5 = **3,024,000**

Fraction: Divide by the total number of books of the bible.

3,024,000 ÷ 66 = **45,818.18 or 45,818 12/66 or 45,818 2/11**

Answers

Activity #5

<u>**F A I T H F U L**</u>
6 1 9 20 8 6 21 12

Addition:

6 + 1 + 9 + 20 + 8 + 6 + 21 + 12 = **<u>83</u>**

Division: divide the total of numbers by the answer.

<u>83</u> ÷ 8 = **10.37**

Subtraction:

6 − 1 − 9 − 20 − 8 − 6 − 21 − 12 = **<u>-71</u>**

Number of Line: Find the answer on the number line.

Multiplication:

6 x 1 x 9 x 20 x 8 x 6 x 21 x 12 = **<u>13,063,680</u>**

Fraction: Place the answer in a fraction form with 66 as the denominator.

<u>13,063,680</u> ÷ 66 = **<u>1,979,345.54 or 1,979,345</u>**

Answers

Activity #6

E P H E S U S
5 16 8 5 19 21 19

Addition:

5 + 16 + 8 + 5 + 19 + 21 + 19 = **93**

Division: Divide the number by the answer.

93 ÷ 7 = 13.28 or 13 2/7

Subtraction:

5 − 16 − 8 − 5 − 19 − 21 − 19 = **−83**

Number Line: Find the number on the number line.

Multiplication:

5 x 16 x 8 x 5 x 19 x 21 x 19 = **24,259,200**

Fraction: Place the answer in a fraction with the total number of books of the bible as the denominator.

24,259,200 ÷ 66 = 367,563.63 or 367,563 42/66 or 367,563 7/11

Answers

Activity #7

CANDLESTICKS
8 1 14 4 12 5 19 20 9 3 11 19

Addition:

8 + 1 + 14 + 12 + 5 + 19 + 20 + 9 + 3 + 11 + 19 = **121**

Division: Divide answer by the total of numbers by added.

121 ÷ 11 = **11**

Subtraction:

8 − 1 − 14 − 12 − 5 − 19 − 20 − 9 − 3 − 11 − 19 = **-105**

Number Line: Find answer on number line.

Multiplication:

8 x 1 x 14 x 12 x 5 x 19 x 20 x 9 x 3 x 11 x 19 = **1,440,996,400**

Decimal: Place answer in decimal form with the total number of books of the bible as the denominator.

1,440,996,400 ÷ 66 = **21833278.79**

Answers

Activity #8

C L O T H E S
3 12 15 20 8 5 19

Addition:

3 + 12 + 15 + 20 + 8 + 5 + 19 = **82**

Division: Divide the number by the total numbers be added to the answer.

82 ÷ 7 = **11.71 and 11 5/7**

Subtraction:

3 − 12 − 15 − 20 − 8 − 5 − 19 = **−76**

Number line: Find the number on the number line.

Multiplication:

3 x 12 x 15 x 20 x 8 x 5 x 19 = **8,208,000**

Decimal: Place the answer in decimal form with the total number of books of the bible as the denominator.

8,208,000 ÷ 66 = **124,363.64**

Answers

Activity #9

<u>S E V E N</u>
19 5 22 5 14

Addition:

19 + 5 + 22 + 5 + 14 = **<u>65</u>**

Division: Divide the number of numbers by the total

<u>65</u> ÷ 4 = **<u>16.25 or 16 1/4</u>**

Subtraction:

19 − 5 − 22 − 5 − 14 = **<u>-27</u>**

Number Line: Find the answer on the number line.

Multiplication:

19 x 5 x 22 x 5 x 4 = **<u>41,800</u>**

Fraction: Place the answer in a fraction with the total number of books of the bible as the denominator.

<u>41,800</u> ÷ 66 = **<u>633.33 or 633 22÷66 or 633 2/6 or 633 1/3</u>**

Answers

Activity #10

F U R N A C E
6 21 18 14 1 3 5

Addition:

6 + 21 + 18 + 14 + 1+ 14 + 3 + 5= **82**

Division: Divide the total of numbers by the answer.

82 ÷ 7 = **11.71 or 11 5/7**

Subtraction:

6 – 21 – 18 – 14 – 1 – 3 – 5= **-56**

Number Line: Find the number on the number line.

Multiplication:

6 x 21 x 18 x 14 x 1 x 3 x 5 = **476,280**

Fraction: Place number in a fraction form with the total number books of the bible as the denominator.

476,280 ÷ 66 = **7,216.36 or 7,216 9/25**

Answers

Activity #11

<u>R U T H</u>
18 21 20 8

Addition:

18 + 21 + 20 + 8 = **67**

Division: Divide by the total of numbers by the answer.

67 ÷ 4 = **16.75 or 16¾**

Subtraction:

18 − 21 − 20 − 8 = **-31**

Number Line: Find the answer on the number line.

Multiplication:

18 x 21 x 20 x 8 = **60,480**

Fraction:
60,480 ÷ 66 = **916.36 or 916 24/66 or 916 4/11**

Answers

Activity #12

M A R Y
13 1 18 25

Addition:

13 + 1 + 18 + 25 = **57**

Division: Divide the number of numbers with the total.

57 ÷ 4 = **14.25 or 14 1/4**

Subtraction:

13 − 1 − 18 − 25 = **−31**

Number Line: Find the number on the number line.

Multiplication:

13 x 1 x 18 x 25 = **5,850**

Fraction: Place the answer in fraction from with the total number of books in the bible as the denominator.

5,850 ÷ 66 = **88.64 or 88 42/66 or 88 7/11**

Answers

Activity #13

M O S E S
13 15 19 5 19

Addition:

13 + 15 + 19 + 5 + 19 = **71**

Division: Divide the number of numbers with answer.

71 ÷ 5 = **14.20 or 14 1/5**

Subtraction:

13 − 15 − 19 − 5 − 19 = **-45**

Number Line: Find answer on the number line.

Multiplication:

13 x 15 x 19 x 5 x 19 = **351,975**

Fraction: Place the answer in a fraction. Use the total of number of books of the bible as a denominator.

351,975 ÷ 66 = **5,332.95 or 5,332 63/66 or 5332 9/11**

Answers

Activity #14

O	B	A	D	I	A	H
15	2	1	4	9	1	8

Addition:

$$15 + 2 + 1 + 4 + 9 + 1 + 8 = \underline{\mathbf{40}}$$

Division: Divide the answer by the total of numbers that is being used.

$$40 \div 7 = \underline{\mathbf{5.71 \text{ or } 5\ 5/7}}$$

Subtraction:

$$15 - 2 - 1 - 4 - 9 - 1 - 8 = \underline{\mathbf{-10}}$$

Number Line: Find the answer on the number line.

Multiplication:

$$15 \times 2 \times 1 \times 4 \times 9 \times 1 \times 8 = \underline{\mathbf{8,640}}$$

Fraction: Place the answer in a fraction using the total of books in the bible.

$$8,640 \div 66 = \underline{\mathbf{130.91 \text{ or } 130\ 60/66}}$$
$$\underline{\mathbf{or\ 130\ 10/11}}$$

Answers

Activity #15

<u>A R K</u>
1 18 11

Addition:

1 + 18 + 11= **<u>30</u>**

Division: Divide the answer to the total of number being added.

30 ÷ 3 = **<u>10</u>**

Subtraction:

1 − 18 − 11= **<u>-28</u>**

Number Line: Find the answer on the number line.

Multiplication:

1 x 18 x 11= **198**

Fractions: Use the answer in a fraction with the total of bible of books as the devisor.

198 ÷ 66 = **<u>3</u>**

Answers

Activity #16

<u>**J E S U S**</u>
10 5 19 21 19

Addition:

10 + 5 + 19 + 21 + 19 = **<u>74</u>**

Division: Divide the number of numbers with answer.

74 ÷ 5 = **<u>14.80 and 14 4/5</u>**

Subtraction:

10 − 5 − 19 − 21 − 19 = **<u>-54</u>**

Number Line: Find the number on the number line.

Multiplication:

10 x 5 x 19 x 21 x 19 = **<u>379,050</u>**

Fractions: Place the answer in a fraction using the total of books of the bible as the denominator.

379,050 ÷ 66 = **<u>5,743.18 or 5743 12/66 or 5,743 2/11</u>**

Answers

Activity #17

```
 I   S   A  I  A  H
 9  19   1  9  1  8
```

Addition:

$$9 + 19 + 1 + 9 + 1 + 8 = \underline{\mathbf{47}}$$

Division: Divide the total number to the answer.

$$\underline{47} \div 6 = \underline{\mathbf{7.83 \text{ or } 7\ 5/6}}$$

Subtraction:

$$9 - 19 - 1 - 9 - 1 - 8 = \underline{\mathbf{-29}}$$

Number Line: Find the answer on the number line.

Multiplication:

$$9 \times 19 \times 1 \times 9 \times 1 \times 8 = \mathbf{12{,}312}$$

Fraction: Place the answer in a fraction with total number of books in the bible as the denominator.

$$\underline{12{,}312} \div 66 = \underline{\mathbf{186.55 \text{ or } 186\ 36/66}}$$
$$\underline{\mathbf{or\ 186\ 6/11}}$$

Answers

Activity #18

<u>M A T T H E W</u>
13 1 20 20 8 5 23

Addition:

13 + 1 + 20 + 20 + 8 + 5 + 23 = **<u>90</u>**

Division: Divide the number of numbers to the answer.

<u>90</u> ÷ 7 = **<u>12.86 and 12 6/7</u>**

Subtraction:

13 − 1 − 20 − 20 − 8 − 5 − 23 = **<u>-64</u>**

<u>Number Line:</u> Find the answer on the number line.

<u>Multiplication:</u>

13 x 1 x 20 x 20 x 8 x 5 x 23 = **<u>4,784,000</u>**

<u>Fraction:</u> Place the answer in a fraction using the total of books of the bible as the denominator.

<u>4,784,000</u> ÷ 66 = **<u>72484.85 or 72,484 56/66 or 72,484 28/33</u>**

Answers

Activity #19

H O S E A
8 15 19 5 1

Addition:

$$8 + 15 + 19 + 5 + 1 = \underline{\mathbf{48}}$$

Division: Divide the total numbers added to the answer.

$$\underline{48} \div 5 = \underline{\mathbf{9.60 \text{ or } 9\ 3/5}}$$

Subtraction:

$$8 - 15 - 19 - 5 - 1 = \underline{\mathbf{-32}}$$

Number of Line: Find the answer on the number line.

Multiplication:

$$8 \times 15 \times 19 \times 5 \times 1 = \underline{\mathbf{11,400}}$$

Fraction: Place the answer in a fraction use the total of books of the bible.

$$\underline{\mathbf{11,400}} \div 66 = \underline{\mathbf{172.73 \text{ or } 172\ 48/66 \text{ or } 172\ 8/11}}$$

Answers

Activity #20

A D A M
1 4 1 13

Addition:

$$1 + 4 + 1 + 13 = \underline{\mathbf{19}}$$

Division: Divide the total of number with the answer.

$$\underline{19} \div 4 = \underline{\mathbf{4.75 \text{ and } 4\ 3/4}}$$

Subtraction:

$$1 - 4 - 1 - 13 = \underline{\mathbf{-17}}$$

Number Line: Find the answer on the number line.

Multiplication:

$$1 \times 4 \times 1 \times 13 = \mathbf{52}$$

Fraction: Place the answer in a fraction with the total of books of the bible as the denominator.

$$\underline{52} \div 66 = \underline{\mathbf{0.78 \text{ or } 26/33}}$$

Answers

Activity #21

<u>**E Z E K I E L**</u>
5 26 5 11 9 5 12

Addition:

5 + 26 + 5 + 11 + 9 + 5 + 12 = **73**

Division:

73 ÷ 7 = **10.43**

Subtraction:

5 − 26 − 5 − 11 − 9 − 5 − 12 = **<u>-63</u>**

Number Line: Find the answer on the number line.

Multiplication:

5 x 26 x 5 x 11 x 9 x 5 x 12 = **<u>3,861,000</u>**

Fraction: Place the answer in a fraction using the total of books in the bible as the denominator.

3,861,000 ÷ 66 = **<u>58,500</u>**

Answers

Activity #22

R	**O**	**M**	**A**	**N**	**S**
18	15	13	1	14	19

Addition:

18 + 5 + 13 + 1 + 14 + 19 = **70**

Division: Divide the total of numbers with the answer.

70 ÷ 6 = **11.67 or 11 4/6 or 11 2/3**

Subtraction:

18 − 5 − 13 − 1 − 14 − 19 = **-34**

Number Line: Find the answer on the number line.

Multiplication:

18 x 5 x 13 x 1 x 14 x 19 = **311,220**

Fraction: Place in a fraction using the total of books of the bible.

311,220 ÷ 66 = **4,715.45 or 4,715 30/66 or 4,715 10/22 or 4,715 5/11**

Answers

Activity #23

J O S E P H
10 15 19 5 16 8

Addition:

10 + 15 + 19 + 16 + 8 = **68**

Division: Divide the answer into the total numbers being added.

68 ÷ 5 = **13.60 or 13 3/5**

Subtraction:

10 − 15 − 19 − 16 − 8 = **−48**

Number Line: Find answer on number line.

Multiplication:

10 x 15 x 19 x 16 x 8 = **364,800**

Fraction: Place the answer in a faction. Use the total number of books in the bible as the denominator.

364,800 ÷ 66 = **5,527.27 or 5527 18/66 or 5527 3/11**

Answers

Activity #24

P S A L M
16 19 1 12 13

Addition:

16 + 19 + 1 + 12 + 13 = **61**

Division: Divide answer into the total number used to add.

61 ÷ 5 = **12.20 or 12 1/5**

Subtraction:

16 − 19 − 1 − 12 − 13 = **−29**

Number Line: Find the number on the number line.

Multiplication:

16 × 19 × 1 × 12 × 13 = **47,424**

Fraction: Place the answer in a fraction using the total number of the books of the bible.

47,424 ÷ 66 = **718.55 or 718 36÷66 or 718 6/11**

Answers

Activity #25

<u>**A B A H**</u>
1 2 1 8

Addition:

$1 + 2 + 1 + 8 =$ **<u>12</u>**

Division: Divide the total of numbers by the answer.

<u>12</u> $\div 4 =$ **<u>3</u>**

Subtraction:

$1 - 2 - 1 - 8 =$ **<u>-10</u>**

Number Line: Find the number on the number line.

Multiplication:

$1 \times 2 \times 1 \times 8 =$ **<u>16</u>**

Fraction: Place answer in a fraction using the total books of the bible.

<u>16</u> $\div 66 =$ **<u>8/33</u>**

Answers

Activity #26

J U D A H
10 21 4 1 8

Addition:

$$10 + 21 + 4 + 1 + 8 = \underline{\mathbf{44}}$$

Division: Divide the total of numbers by the answer.

$$44 \div 5 = \underline{\mathbf{8.80 \text{ or } 8\ 4/5}}$$

Subtraction:

$$10 - 21 - 4 - 1 - 8 = \underline{\mathbf{-24}}$$

Number Line: Find the number on the number line.

Multiplication:

$$10 \times 21 \times 4 \times 1 \times 8 = \underline{\mathbf{6{,}720}}$$

Fraction: Place the answer in a fraction using the total of books in the bible as the denominator.

$$6{,}720 \div 66 = \underline{\mathbf{101.82 \text{ or } 101\ 54/66 \text{ or } 101\ 9/11}}$$

Answers

Activity #27

J O H N
10 15 8 14

Addition:

10 + 15 + 8 + 4 = **37**

Division: Divide the total numbers by the answer.

37 ÷ 4 = **9.25 or 9 1/4**

Subtraction:

10 − 15 − 8 − 4 = **-17**

Number Line: Find the answer on the number line.

Multiplication:

10 x 15 x 8 x 4 = **4,800**

Fraction: Place the answer in the fraction using the total number of books in the bible.

4,800 ÷ 66 = **72.73 or 72 48/66 or 72 8/11**

Answers

Activity #28

<u>**A M O S**</u>
1 13 15 19

Addition:

1 + 13 + 15 + 19 = **<u>48</u>**

Division: Divide the total of number with the answer.

48 ÷ 4 = **<u>12</u>**

Subtraction:

1 − 13 − 15 − 19 = **<u>−46</u>**

Number Line: Find the number on the number line.

Multiplication:

1 x 13 x 15 x 19 = **<u>3,705</u>**

Fraction: Place the answer in a fraction using the total of books in the bible as the denominator.

<u>3,705</u> ÷ 66 = **<u>56.14 or 56 9/66 or 56 3/22</u>**

Answers

Animals In The Bible

Directions: Break the code by using the number chart above. Once you have broken the code, add, divide and reduce to lowest fraction and place in decimal from, subtract, identify on number line, multiple, and divide and find the lowest common fraction. After coding find words in puzzle.

$$\frac{A}{1} \quad \frac{B}{2} \quad \frac{C}{3} \quad \frac{D}{4} \quad \frac{E}{5} \quad \frac{F}{6} \quad \frac{G}{7} \quad \frac{H}{8} \quad \frac{I}{9}$$

$$\frac{J}{10} \quad \frac{K}{11} \quad \frac{L}{12} \quad \frac{M}{13} \quad \frac{N}{14} \quad \frac{O}{15} \quad \frac{P}{16} \quad \frac{Q}{17} \quad \frac{R}{18}$$

$$\frac{S}{19} \quad \frac{T}{20} \quad \frac{U}{21} \quad \frac{V}{22} \quad \frac{W}{23} \quad \frac{X}{24} \quad \frac{Y}{25} \quad \frac{Z}{26}$$

Answers

C	C	H	R	I	S
B	A	F	I	S	H
I	S	L	L	U	B
R	P	A	V	L	E
D	S	C	Q	E	Y
S	N	C	V	L	S
E	I	E	I	A	G
C	O	R	W	M	O
I	L	D	H	B	D
M	C	E	O	E	Z
E	A	L	R	T	A
L	E	G	S	F	E
B	W	A	E	L	C
I	E	E	D	W	R
B	J	A	W	O	O

75

Answers

Activity #31

<u>C A L V E S</u>
3 1 12 22 5 19

Addition:

3 + 1 + 12 + 22 + 5 + 12 = **55**

Division:

55 ÷ 6 = **9.17 or 9 1/6**

Subtraction:

3 − 1 − 12 − 22 − 5 − 12 = **−49**

Multiplication:

3 × 12 × 22 × 5 × 12 = **47,520**

Fraction:

47,520 ÷ 66 = **720**

Answers

Activity #32

<u>C A L   F</u>
3 1 12 6

Addition:

3 + 1 + 12 + 6 = **22**

Division:

22 ÷ 66 = **11/33 or 1/3**

Subtraction:

3 − 1 − 12 − 6 = *-14*

Multiplication:

3 x 1 x 12 x 6 = **216**

Fraction:

216 ÷ 66 = **3.27 or 3 18/66 or 3 3/11**

Answers

Activity #33

B	**E**	**A**	**S**	**T**
2	5	1	19	20

Addition:

2 + 5 + 1 + 19 + 20 = **47**

Division:

47 ÷ 5 = **9.40 or 9 2/5**

Subtraction:

2 − 5 − 1 − 19 − 20 = **-43**

Multiplication:

2 x 5 x 1 x 19 x 20 = **3,800**

Fraction:

3,800 ÷ 66 = **57.58**

Answers

Activity #34

B	**I**	**R**	**D**	**S**
2	9	18	4	19

Addition:

2 + 9 + 18 + 4 + 19 = **52**

Division:

52 ÷ 5 = **10.40 or 10 2/5**

Subtraction:

2 − 9 − 18 − 4 − 19 = **−48**

Multiplication:

2 × 9 × 18 × 4 × 19 = **24,624**

Fraction:

24,624 ÷ 66 = **373.09**

Answers

Activity #35

$$\underline{\textbf{B U L L S}}$$
$$2\ 21\ 12\ 12\ 19$$

Addition:

$$2 + 21 + 22 + 12 + 19 = \underline{\textbf{76}}$$

Division:

$$\underline{\textbf{76}} \div 5 = \underline{\textbf{15.20 or 15 1/5}}$$

Subtraction:

$$2 - 21 - 22 - 12 - 19 = \underline{\textbf{-72}}$$

Multiplication:

$$2 \times 21 \times 22 \times 12 \times 19 = \underline{\textbf{210,672}}$$

Fraction:

$$\underline{\textbf{210,672}} \div 66 = \underline{\textbf{3,192}}$$

Answers

Activity #36

$$\underline{\textbf{D O G}}$$
4 15 7

Addition:

4 + 15 +7 = **26**

Division:

26 ÷ 3 = **8.66**

Subtraction:

4 − 15 − 7 = **-18**

Multiplication:

4 x 15 x 7 = **420**

Fraction:

420 ÷ 66 = **6.36**

Answers

Activity #37

B A G E L
2 1 7 5 12

Addition:

$$2 + 1 + 7 + 12 + 5 = \underline{\mathbf{27}}$$

Division:

$$\underline{27} \div 66 = \underline{\mathbf{9/22}}$$

Subtraction:

$$2 - 1 - 7 - 12 - 5 = \underline{\mathbf{-23}}$$

Multiplication:

$$2 \times 1 \times 7 \times 12 \times 5 = \underline{\mathbf{840}}$$

Fraction:

$\underline{840} \div 66 = \underline{\mathbf{12.73 \text{ or } 12\ 48/66 \text{ or } 12\ 8/11}}$

Answers

Activity #38

<u>E W E</u>
5 23 5

Addition:

5 + 23 + 5 = __33__

Division: Divide the answer above by the number below.

33 ÷ 3 = __11__

Subtraction:

5 − 23 − 5 = __−23__

Multiplication:

5 x 23 x 5 = **575**

Fraction: Convert the answer above into a fraction or decimal using the total number of books in the bible as the devisor.

575 ÷ 66 = **8.71**

Answers

Activity #39

<u>F I S H</u>
6 9 19 8

Addition:

6 + 9 + 19 + 8 = **<u>42</u>**

Division:

<u>42</u> ÷ 4 = **<u>10.50 or 10 2/4 or 10 1/2</u>**

Subtraction:

6 − 9 − 19 − 8 = **<u>−30</u>**

Multiplication:

6 x 9 x 19 x 8 = **<u>8,208</u>**

Fraction:

<u>8,208</u> ÷ 66 = **<u>124.36 or 124 24/66 or 12 4/11</u>**

Answers

Activity #40

<u>**H O R S E**</u>
8 15 18 19 5

Addition:

8 + 15 + 18 + 19 +5 = **<u>65</u>**

Division:

65 ÷ 5 = **<u>13</u>**

Subtraction:

9 − 15 −18 − 19 − 5 = **<u>−48</u>**

Multiplication:

9 x 15 x 18 x 19 x 5 = **<u>230,850</u>**

Fraction:

<u>**230,850**</u> ÷ 66 = **<u>3,497.73 or 3,497 48/66 or 3497 8/11</u>**

Answers

Activity #41

<u>J A W</u>
10 1 23

Addition:

10 + 1 + 23 = **<u>34</u>**

Division:

<u>34</u> ÷ 3 = **<u>11.33 or 11 1/3</u>**

Subtraction:

10 − 1 − 23 = **<u>-14</u>**

Multiplication:

10 x 1 x 23 = **<u>230</u>**

Fraction:

<u>230</u> ÷ 66 = **<u>3.48 or 3 32/66 or 3 12/22 or 3 6/11</u>**

Answers

Activity #42

<u>**L A M B**</u>
12 1 13 2

Addition:

$$12 + 1 + 13 + 2 = \underline{\mathbf{28}}$$

Division:

$$\underline{\mathbf{28}} \div 4 = \underline{\mathbf{7}}$$

Subtraction:

$$12 - 1 - 13 - 2 = \underline{\mathbf{-4}}$$

Multiplication:

$$12 \times 1 \times 13 \times 2 = \underline{\mathbf{312}}$$

Fraction:

$$\underline{\mathbf{312}} \div 66 = \underline{\mathbf{4.75 \text{ or } 4\ 48/66 \text{ or } 4\ 8/11}}$$

Answers

Activity #43

<u>**L   I   O   N   S**</u>
12   9   15   14   19

Addition:

12 + 9 + 15 + 14 + 19 = **69**

Division:

69 ÷ 5 = **13.80 or 13 4/5**

Subtraction:

12 − 15 − 9 − 14 − 19 = **-45**

Multiplication:

12 x 9 x 15 x 14 x 19 = **430,920**

Fraction:

430,920 ÷ 66 = **6,529.09 or 6,529 6/66 or 6,529 1/6**

Answer

Activity #44

<u>**M I C E**</u>
13 9 3 5

Addition:

13 + 9 + 3 + 5 = **<u>30</u>**

Division:

<u>30</u> ÷ 4 = **<u>7.50 or 7 2/4 o r 7 ½</u>**

Subtraction:

13 − 9 − 3 − 5 = **<u>−4</u>**

Multiplication:

13 × 9 × 3 × 5 = **<u>1,755</u>**

Fraction:

<u>1,755</u> ÷ 66 = **<u>26.59 or 26 39/66 or 26 13/22</u>**

ABOUT THE AUTHOR

A native Mississippian, Coretta R. Wren has been inspired to reach out by educating others about the Word of God. Coretta's inspiration comes from twenty years of educating youth as a substitute instructor. Her belief that God provides fruitful life to those who come to know Him caused her to seek an appealing method through which she could teach others and open the door to true wisdom. *"The fear of the Lord is the beginning of wisdom."*

By creatively combining fun and academic methods with biblical content Coretta is providing a tool which increases a person's knowledge of God and His Word. It can be used as an educational resource in various bible schools, youth groups, and Christian education institutions, or for those who simply like learning while they have fun.

To contact Coretta email or call:

Know Me Publications
Email: WrenKnowMePublication@Yahoo.com
Website: www.knowmepubulications.com

Book Order Form

Counting on GOD

Multiplying Math Skills with Spiritual Principles

PLEASE PRINT CLEARLY

Name _____

Address _____

City _____ State _____ Zip _____

Phone _____ Fax _____

Email _____

Quantity	
Price *(each)*	$7.99
Subtotal	
S & H	.99
MI Tax 6%	
Total	

METHOD OF PAYMENT:
❏ Check or Money Order
(Make payable to: Coretta Wren)

❏ Visa   ❏ MasterCard   ❏ American Express

Acct No. _____

Expiration Date (*mmyy*) _____

Signature _____

Mail your payment to:
ATTN: Coretta Wren
PriorityONE Publications
P. O. Box 361332
Grosse Pointe, MI 48236

or call:
248-635-6200

www.ingramcontent.com/pod-product-compliance
Lightning Source LLC
Chambersburg PA
CBHW050604300426
44112CB00013B/2060